Tout comprendre, c'est

tout pardonner:

To understand all, is to forgive all.

By: Ivory Luv

Library of Congress Cataloging – in- Publication Data has been applied for.

PRINTED IN THE UNITED STATES OF AMERICA.

FIRST EDITION

For my sister-in-love

Rayshonda Marie Roberts,

aka Ray Ray,

This is not only for me, but it's for you as well. We talked about our struggles and motivated one another a lot. You treated me like a sister from the day I met you (all my emotions and ups and downs, too), and for that, I will always love you. Although we didn't get a chance to go on our pottery and painting with a twist date, know that I'm still carrying on and fighting on for me and you. Glad I got to spend lots of time with you and love on you. Thank you for being an example of strength in my life.

I love you and miss you a lot, until we meet again, sis.

Acknowledgments

First, I would like to give all praise to God. May He continue to bless me, heal me, and use me for the good.

Kurtis O'neal Graves II, my husband, M4L, the person who came in and showed me another me. Who supported me, loved me, and encouraged me through everything. Thank you for never giving up on me, taking your time with me, and showing me things I could never see in myself. Thank you for protecting me and loving me endlessly. When everyone wanted me to change and be different, you let me know it was okay to be me and that if I was going to change, it needed to be because I wanted to. Thank you for being as frustrated and angry with me through this health and life journey but never letting me feel it. Thank You, Papi; I love You.

Nyiem, K.O., my firstborn, my Sonny. I love you. Thank you for being the best version of you. Thank you for motivating me silently and honestly verbally whenever I slipped up. Thank you for giving me something that no one could ever give me, unconditional love. You learned to cook so that I wouldn't, as my health got a little more challenging. You have been my reason since 2005 when I heard your little heartbeat. You have been my rock. Nothing is by mistake, not you, not us, not your love. Thank you for never making me feel my mistakes or holding them against me. You'll forever be my first love.

Zaynah, my Butta Butt, my Pumpkin. You were a different type of love, but not far from your brother. Thank you for humbling me, challenging and clinging to me. You have challenged me to fix myself and my ways. You always know what to do to make me feel loved; instead, even if it's a card you would make, bath drawn with candles, or even sleeping with me. You have shown me how to be loved without conditions. We bump heads so much because you are just like me, only a little more confident in who you are and driven. Thank you, Princess, for the love that can take me so far. My first daughter, my challenger, I love you.

Mom, Mom, thank you for raising me. Thank you for the tough love and the challenges. Thank you for providing for me. Making sure I stayed on task in school and keeping me active during my childhood years. Most importantly, thank you for getting to know me as an adult and supporting me through my hip surgeries. All the moments we watched TV together, Twilight movies, Greenleaf, Sci-Fi channel, and Underworld, to name a few. You made sure that I was on top of my hydration and the laughing nights we had and for being an example of forgiveness, restarts, and a fresh start at love. You've sacrificed so much for me growing up; I will never forget that. I love you. You are missed very much.

Grandmom Rudine, thank you for always being a light in my life. You showed me so much, like how to be spoiled. "It's so many things I take with me that you have taught me as a little girl, something as little as eating around the sides of my cream of wheat because that's where it was cool enough to eat at first. You also love me unconditionally and always protect me. Our talks are memorable, and I enjoy everything you do for me and talk to me about. I love you.

Thank you to my parents, Lovy and Phil. Thank you for being the first examples of love. Thank you for bringing me into this world and caring for me so deeply. Thanks for the times you went to appointments and surgeries. Y'all have shown me how to press forward, how to never give up, and how to go after whatever I wanted in life, no matter the obstacle. Thank you for being a part of who I have been molded to be. Thank you, Mom, for coming to my rescue numerous times and being a person I can call last minute to come through for me and my kids. Thank you for all that you both do for my kids. I love both of you.

Grandpop Phil and Uncle Billy, thank you for being my first and the very best men who have shown me how to be loved by a man. For showing me how a man is supposed to treat me. Thank you for being an example to me of gentle and intentional love. Both of you have loved me since the very first day I was born. You have never let me down and never broken your promises. Thank you for being everything to me and great examples of Men; I love you both.

Thank you to my In-Loves; thank you for supporting me. Thank you for attending appointments and holding me accountable many times. For listening to me, giving me advice, and allowing me to cry on your shoulders many times. Thank you for loving me. Most importantly, Thank You, Momma Ginger and Pops, for birthing such a great son, someone who I could depend on and who loves me unapologetically.

Nancy & Sig, thank you for helping shape my childhood. Thank you for introducing me to my first favorite book that encouraged me to read more; you're the reason I love reading. Thank you for teaching me how to sew and all of the visits to your house on Thanksgiving, that allowed me to let go and enjoy being a kid. You both came into my life at the perfect time, and I thank you both for that truly.

Thank you to every doctor who has had and has a part to play in my healing and better quality of life. Thank you for being patient with me and kind to me. Thank you to the therapist I have seen and the many nurses, medical assistants, anesthesiologists, and more.

Thank you to my Physical and Occupational Therapists at ATI Physical Therapy Q, Carol, Puja, Lauren, and Barb. Y'all have worked with me, listened to me scream, cry, want to give up, complain and cancel last-minute therapy sessions. Thank you for never giving up on me and motivating me. Thank you for pushing me past limits I thought were in place, and thank you for all the encouragement. Q and Carol thank you for supporting this book long before it was officially published. Q, thank you for being a friend long before ATI; when you were going to school, you helped me along my healing journey, so thank you for that. Thank you, Rich, for picking me up and dropping me off every therapy visit. Even when transportation ended, you found a way to get me there and back; I appreciate you all so much for playing a part in my recovery and healing.

Thank you to all my family and friends who have ever supported me. Whether that was a text, a phone call, visiting me at the hospital, taking me to an appointment, asking about my well-being, or even crying with me. It's way too many to list, but I love you all very much.

Table of Contents

Introduction

I had dreams of the Navy for as long as I can remember. I wanted to be a nurse on the Navy ship. My aunt Sandra was always that dream motivation. I also wanted to become a forensic scientist while being in the Navy. Everything I wanted to be led to me serving and caring for someone. I feel like I've always had a serving bone in my body. I felt so much happiness doing so. That all changed when my life troubles came about. I then started to serve and take care of people a little differently than I originally wanted to...

To anyone reading these words right now, this story isn't a blame game or a woe is me. This is an awareness story. To me, this is a story that tells "The Story" that so many people have and will continue to grow through. The awareness is the consequences and impacts of this recurring story on all of us and the generations that follow in its wake. The awareness expresses the need to break the generational curses that have us trapped. This story is the hope and blessing of someone who is going through but feels like the world doesn't understand. Awareness can't change the past, but it can reshape the narrative and the false beliefs invested in these failed methods, resulting in lasting trauma and damage that must be undone to progress toward a happy and meaningful life.

There's more than one side to each story, and this is mine. Everyone won't relate. Everyone won't agree. To those people, this story may not be for you. I appreciate you reading it and respect your views and feelings even if I disagree with you and you with me. This is not an attention grabber, an opportunity to attack, or a scandalous tell-all. It is simply a story that I hope reaches and helps someone decide to fight on to their future that has the potential to be so much brighter than their present.

Whether you're a struggling child, a confused adolescent, or a full-grown adult struggling to overcome and define the damage done to you (whether maliciously or inadvertently) during your youth, with the hopes of healing yourself and others in your life, this is your story. As someone struggling daily with numerous traumas and tragedies at 34 years of age, I say to you that you aren't alone and that seeking healing for yourself and others is not a lost cause. If nothing else, healing yourself is the most honorable thing you can do and the best way to benefit the people who depend on and care for you.

To the people who feel like no one like that exists in your life, I assure you that isn't true.

Reach out to me, ivorygraves427@gmail.com, and you'll find out that someone on this earth cares about your next breath and hopes to witness and be a part of the joy and happiness in your life. Please keep valuing yourself. You matter. Your life may have been difficult beyond bearing before you picked up this book, but now that you have it, you have a friend. You have resources available to start making a change in your life today. Everything that has happened to you has happened for a reason. I can't tell you the reason, but we can explore it together.

EVERYTHING HAPPENS FOR A REASON
Ain't No Buts...

My Truth

I grew up in an overcrowded home. There were nine of us to start, one baby on the way, and my two adopted aunts came later, increasing the number. We were cared for by my overtaxed and overextended maternal grandmother. Though she did her very best to make sure our every physical need was met, she expressed her frustration, anger, and disappointment in hurtful and abusive ways.

Growing up, there was a lot happening in my overcrowded home. I remember times of having the gas cut off. My grandmother cooked meals on a hot plate. We stayed in one room together because we only had a portable heater big enough for one room. The house was big, three stories, to be exact. We had to boil water on the hot plate to fill up a blue bucket to take baths in. We didn't change the water as we took baths. I'm guessing because it took so long to fill up, that was easiest.

I would run to the bathroom because it was cold, and I wanted to return to the warm room. Sometimes I even held it. We ate one pot of oodles of noodles, one pot of spaghetti, or something that was easy to make. We survived.

During that time, I'm not sure I realized the extent of how bad things were. We had bad roaches and rats running in the ceiling. We had fleas in the basement from pets, so bad that when you went down with white socks, they were black when you came up. That's actually how we checked to see if our flea treatment was working or not. These things were handled eventually, and as kids, we just went on with life; that was the norm. I know it didn't feel good, but what was I really to do as a kid?

We often went to the Whosoever Gospel Mission, which my grandmother called the "fill a bag." She called it this because she was able to fill a brown paper bag for $1 with anything she wanted to put in it. I remember helping my grandmother look through clothes, roll them tight, and stuff brown paper bags with items for me, my siblings, and even my cousins. She even got into arguments and shoving matches to get things she had or things she had her eyes on. Those were the days.

I was often ignored because it was a crowded house. Not ignored, meaning when I talked, no one talked back, or when I went to someone, I wasn't answered. Ignored in the sense of feeling invisible. The things I struggled with, I kept to myself because I felt I had no choice but to do so. As a kid back then, you didn't really have "problems," you just stayed a kid, stayed out of grown folks' business, and did what you were told. If you had any issues, it was dismissed or ignored because you were a kid.

Early on, I remember getting in trouble for a lot of things, whether that was fighting my sibling, getting a hole in my stocking, talking in class, or even getting water on the bathroom floor. I also remember being called names, which my siblings called me as well. Don't get me wrong, I called names as well and was an angry little girl, but I struggled a lot because of these things. I was being called names like "40 cent," "Big Forehead," and others.

My mouth (talking back) got me into trouble as well. I just don't think the things I got in trouble for should have been so severe. I was popped in my mouth, to which my lip was busted, and I was beaten with a belt. I feel as though my biological sister was favored over me, so that was also something that made me angry growing up. It made me feel worthless and like I barely mattered in the family and life. It also caused me to self-inflict and contemplate suicide; I'll get into detail about this later in the chapter *Mental Health*.

I had a little escape, the Drill Team. The Drill Team provided us with a way to do something we all liked to do. We stayed out of trouble because of it. I enjoyed it a lot. When it was practice and competition time, I loved it because I didn't focus on home life. I was also good at competing, but when everyone left, it was back to reality. So that was only a temporary fix for me.

Other escapes I had were the ballet, jazz, and hip-hop classes I took as a child, going to the library because I absolutely loved to read, and even the fire hydrant on the corner of our block being turned on. We went to Water View Recreation Center and different camps during the summer. My grandmother made all of our outfits for the drill team and even some stuff for the ballet and jazz performances. So, I had some good times as a child too, but they were still just temporary fixes.

She encouraged me to sew when she made our outfits. I sewed a little and made my first dress when I was about 12. It was a sundress that was purple with flowers. Nancy taught me, though; I'll explain who Nancy is later.

I took Piano and violin lessons and wasn't too bad at playing them either. I played the violin in school shows. One of the concerts I will never forget is a Scotland one we did, and someone from Scotland came. I still remember that day and how different and exciting it was. Through these things I did as a child, I masked how I felt, enjoyed the activities in those moments, and went on waiting for the next escape adventure to arrive.

Going through the abuse in my childhood, I thought so very ill and little of myself. I felt I deserved all the abuse and that I was ugly. I didn't think I deserved to be treated any better than I was being treated. Sometimes, I would wonder what life would be like if I lived with one of my parents. I dreamt of constant family dinners, happy times, being spoiled, and lots of continuous fun. I mean, we had Thanksgiving and Christmas gatherings with my family, but I wanted the in-home mom and dad dinners. Maybe some bad days but nothing like I had to endure living in the home I grew up in.

Nobody knew about any of these behaviors and incidents. I carried it with me for many years – until now. I do wish my grandmother was still here because I have so many questions to ask her, to just understand her better. Why did she seem so angry all the time? Why didn't she do anything for herself? What made her take us in? Did she regret anything she'd done for me and for herself? How was her childhood and upbringing? And so much more.

I went through so much at a young age that it partially broke me and made me do things that I didn't particularly like and agree with. But today, the truth is that it gave me the strength I have today. Sometimes in life, we often suppress the truth because of other people's feelings and the fear of how they will be viewed. But all in all, the truth is the truth. Worrying about how someone will view you does not change the truth.

My maternal grandmother, whom I now realize had no space for herself and never had a break, did the best she could. She went from raising her children to me and my siblings, who are her daughters' children, to then having two foster kids she adopted very early on. So, when did she ever have time to grow and learn better?

Abuse

buse, whether physical, emotional, or even verbal, is harmful and causes issues in your life and through your relationships. With me, it started as a little girl. I experienced some mistreatment and abuse. I wanted to be rescued. I did a lot in my life to be praised but never received it. I wasn't perfect at all. My maternal grandmother raised me until I was about 15 years old.

While in the house, I busied myself with reading, writing, and even puzzles. I danced sometimes as well. It all gave me little mental escapes. I also drew often. Figures, clothes, and even just a bunch of lines all over the paper and coloring in the little spaces. I loved anything that showed my creativity. I made clothes out of things I found around the house and just knew I was it, *that girl!*

Can you believe I made a purse out of Capri Sun pouches? I cut up basketball and football jerseys and shirts and made them outfits as well; these things were fun. Around this time, I started doing hair as well. First, on my baby dolls, and then eventually on to my friends. I would sometimes watch my grandmother, Aunt Penda, and God Mom Tara do hair.

The freedom of expression through hair was what I loved about it. It gave people a different look and smile after getting out of the chair. When I got a little older, I drew a picture of a mobile hair salon. I wanted to take appointments in different neighborhoods. I wanted to run sales and give back by doing hair for the girls going back to school. I wrote out details of this mobile salon and everything that somehow never happened back to where we were.

During these younger years, I was then fondled by someone. I believe I got in trouble or was upset about something, and I was sent to my room. He made his way to my room, sat me on his lap, and kissed my cheek. Rubbed my arm and leg and told me it would be okay and to stop crying. He told me I was pretty and that he would be with me if I was older.

When he started dating someone older, I was jealous and mad. Me a kid, jealous – that wasn't normal behavior, but at that time, it felt normal to me. He showed me something I was missing in my life, attention. I realized it wasn't normal or okay when I got older; it actually made me angry in a different way. I never mentioned anything to anyone because I wasn't sure anyone would believe me. Remember, I felt invisible anyway. However, it seems like after that; I fell into a pattern of being abused in some way.

I later met the birth father of my son. The first few months were great. Quickly after that "honeymoon phase," I went through physical and verbal abuse with him. When I was pregnant with my son, my mother didn't want to take care of a pregnant teen. At the time, she was going through a divorce, so I'm sure that was a lot to deal with at the same time as me deciding to keep my baby.

I started living with my son's birth father. There I suffered a black eye, was slapped time and time again, and was called names. All of this stemmed from him being caught cheating or even me standing up for myself in trying to have fairness in the relationship. Mentally it was a lot, but I stayed. Why, you ask? I wanted to prove everybody wrong about being a young and soon-to-be single teen mom. They also said the relationship wouldn't last long and it would be hard.

A lot of these people saw things I didn't see or that I shielded myself from wanting to see. I just wanted it to work, but the cheating, manipulation, and abuse became too much. Going to summer school with a black eye and lying about it should have been my eye-opener long before I became pregnant, but my last straw was being dragged down the steps with my son in my arms and put outside because I caught him cheating.

My mom came to his house so fast and caused a scene. She had her best friend, G-Mom, with her. She scooped us up and took us back to her house. We really didn't discuss much of it after that. I was upset that my baby boy had to witness this; though he was young, I was so sure he would have memories of it. But that was it for me, or was it? Well, for him, it was.

My father verbally abused me. He never put his hands on me, but he never had sweet words to say. Many times in my late teens to adulthood, he called me out of my name or told me I wasn't going to be sh*t. He told me someone else should knock my head off, using my abuse trauma against me. He wasn't anybody I could run to if I wanted to because I felt he was no different from other abusers.

I remember telling him about my son's birth father, and he told me, "Well, you have cousins, tell them."

I knew after that I couldn't go to him about anything. There was no safety there. He has left nasty, threatening messages on my voicemail. My cousin had to even go to his house because of the things that were said and how aggressive he was toward me. We struggled to have a relationship all of my young adult and adult life. Things seemed to pick up here and there, and then we were right back in a cycle of not speaking and being distant.

I am hoping that the pattern breaks one day. To be honest, I see him getting older, and I would love to have a stable relationship with him one day. Until then...

My daughter's birth father did the same as my son's birth father four years later. Same cycle, different person. The very first time I remember being abused was because I got sick in school and needed to go to the hospital. My blood pressure was dropping, and my heart rate was high. My teachers, who were nurses, insisted on me going because of how dizzy I was and how my numbers looked. Instead, he wanted to go hang out and go swimming. He was insistent on me going later after he was done.

When we were on the highway, I was telling my mom what was going on and that he wasn't going to take me to be checked out. He pulled over onto the shoulder of the road, snatched my phone out of my hand, and threw it in the trunk. He then drove to my house, which was about two hours away.

He locked the door as soon as we got into the house, and I was scared at that point. I told my son to go to his room, and I went to mine. He followed us up the stairs. He locked the door and put the mattress on it. I was punched, slapped, and slammed on a wood slack bed (you know, those platform beds that don't require a box spring mattress?).

I was kicked and blacked out from the slam on the platform frame. When I came back to complete consciousness, I tried to run. I ran to the window, opened it, and screamed. He slammed it shut. I tried to stay away from him as much as I could, but the room was pretty small.

I heard my son crying from the next room, but I couldn't get to him. I just wanted to get to my son and console him. I wanted him to know that Mommy was okay. The thing that saved me was my mom banging on the door. She knew something had to be wrong after the phone hung up and she drove two hours to my house.

My mom banged on the door, and somehow something switched inside him. The rage and anger I saw in his eyes disappeared. I can't lie; I thought someone called the cops. I believe he did, too, until I saw my mom's car out of the window. He let me out of the room as if nothing happened.

I went downstairs and my mom saw the tears, whelps, and more. She had my G-mom with her again. They were enraged. They were arguing with him. My son then said he heard everything, and he was crying so badly. I was sick; that hurt me more than how I was physically, emotionally, and mentally feeling. Here I thought and was upset that he would remember what happened with his birth father as a baby, but he had to endure and remember this.

I went to the hospital, but I never pressed charges. Weeks later, I found out I was pregnant, *and then* I returned to him when I was five months pregnant. I experienced abuse again. He would make me sleep without a blanket, and I would have to sleep on the floor because I had a cold. I was shoved into the wall when I tried to leave; my son was with me and witnessed this again.

That was it for me. I called my mother, who came with G-mom again (they really always came to my rescue); I walked out and was done. For good this time.

I'm not proud of this, but this is a part of my story. I was never supposed to go back to both birth fathers, but I did, and when I did, I ended up pregnant both times. I didn't want to be just a baby mother. I wanted my kids to have a two-parent household and to build a family of my own. Growing up, I didn't have that, and I didn't want that for my children.

I wanted my children to have everything I didn't have growing up and more, just not at the expense of being hurt and abused over and over again or undervalued and unappreciated. It was the best and safest choice for me and my babies. My daughter's birth father was never really there, and my son's was in and out. Eventually, they both faded out on their own, and I did it by myself until my husband, and I rekindled our relationship years later.

I don't have any regrets, though, and I don't hold any ill will toward my children's birth fathers or my own father. I'm grateful I met them because I have two beautiful children, and my father gave me life. They were lessons, and I have blessings from what I endured.

Sometimes, we don't get to choose our circumstances, but we can make choices to better our outcome, and that's just what I did. My children now see a healthy home and have a steady and very present father.

Daddy Issues

I n my younger years, my father was very present. A little while ago, I listened to him and my mom tell me stories of times he would come to get me and how it would be when I went over to my grandparent's house (his parents), My Aunt Ellen's, or even my Aunt Rosie house on Easter or to see her. It's memories I don't remember, so it was refreshing to hear. My mom told me how he always picked me up and came to my drill team competitions. I remember he drove to Ohio to see me perform. It seemed like he was kept from interacting with me consistently, however. He told me he would come and try and get me every other weekend but was told "No" due to Drill Team practice and competitions—other times, just "No." I was not aware.

The times he did get me, I went to his house. We had seafood, I played games, and I played with the neighbor kids across the street. My father would buy me what I wanted for my birthday; what I asked for, he got. It seemed like he eventually faded away. Maybe he gave up when he came to get me, and I couldn't go with him. That had to be hard.

I didn't hear from him as much or sometimes not at all. I wasn't invited to his wedding and I'm unsure who decision that was, but it stopped shortly after that. He would make promises and not follow through or wouldn't answer my calls. I remember waiting up for him many times and eventually falling asleep or being told to go on to bed.

When he was present in my life as a young adult and adult, he made promises that he never kept repeating the same cycle. I went through a lot with my father. In the summer of 2015, he embarrassed me at our family reunion in front of some of our family members.

It was a relief for me in a way, but so much more hurt came with it. I thought we had moved past this and that all was forgiven from our past and how he treated me the previous years. We talked, and I thought he understood where he went wrong, and I admitted how I could have and would be better. I guess not.

I wanted my family to know what I've been going through with him for years, but I never wanted them to find out in this manner. It took me back to hating him as I did before, and indeed it showed his true colors. Everyone saw exactly how he treated me and heard what he thought of me as his daughter. I have no actual words to express or describe my feelings, our relationship, or the lack thereof.

I can think of so many reasons why I felt this way early on. I clearly remember Jr. prom. Of course, most girls in high school (some even in middle school) look forward to prom day. When the time came to plan for Jr. Prom, he included himself in the big day. He told me he wanted to help and asked how much I needed, and then agreed on the amount. Long story short, the day came, and he was a no-show.

After getting our prom tickets, I got out of school early on the day of prom. He wasn't answering the phone, and he never called back either. The money he offered was supposed to go to my hair, nails, and flowers, so you can understand my frustration. I called from different numbers, and my mother even called, and nope, no answer; now it was going straight to voicemail.

I was furious! I cried so much and said I wasn't going anymore. He always stood me up, and I always made excuses for him or gave him a pass, but this time was different. This was so important to me. I couldn't forgive him for this. To talk to me all week about these plans and repeat them each conversation and then stand me up the very day was just unacceptable.

It was just the beginning of me realizing it and no longer accepting it or making excuses for his actions. Thank God for my girlfriend Tia's mother and my Aunt Jo because they saved the day. Tia's mother got my nails and feet done while my Aunt Jo came last minute to slay my hair; thank you so much for this, by the way.

Another thing that put a dent in us was finding out I had a brother in my early teens. It made me feel jealous, and we were distant much more. He always visited my brother, and he would tell me he was going there. My brother and I lived down the street from each other, but I didn't receive visits as often as he did. I'm sure he would say he was catching up, but in my eyes, we needed to catch up too. He didn't get it though.

For years and years, I wanted my father's side of the family to understand what was going on with us. I thought I dropped what I would call "hints." But what I later found was that I was presented to be a teenager just going through "teenage things." I was also a teenage mother, so maybe they thought I was "smelling myself," I don't know.

It was hard to get someone to believe that I wasn't and that these kinds of things were going on, so I distanced myself because of it. I have never liked to feel as if I have to prove myself. In that environment, I very well felt that I did. I just wanted a great relationship with my father.

He told them over the years that I was disrespectful and kept my children from him. Also, I didn't want to be around his family or attend events. I was never told about any of these events, and the times he didn't see my children were times we weren't speaking. The lies had to stop somehow in some way, and I was tired of being blindsided by him. Now you can kind of understand where the relief of the family reunion blow-up came from. I was verbally abused by my father, but that day I also grew a closer bond with some family members, whom I would say were just not sure if the things they were told were true up until this point.

No, no one ever asked my side. They just took his word and stories. Some still do, but at this point, it's water under the bridge. I am so used to it and over it that apologies don't matter at this point. Those years of verbal abuse, his being absent and not supportive, are gone.

I can't get back the years of events that I missed with my family or being around them. I just don't care to dwell on that at this point. I want to move forward. We still don't have a stable relationship, and I'm starting to feel like it's better that way. If it changes, it changes; if it doesn't, then it doesn't. You can only change yourself, not the status of a person and their actions.

So many times, as women, we don't realize how much we need our fathers. We don't even realize sometimes how much of them not being around affects our decision-making regarding guys, cars, or anything. Even now, sometimes, I cry because he isn't around in a positive sense for me. I have to learn by myself what to accept and what not to accept in relationships and how a man should even love me.

When you have to learn on your own, it takes so long to figure out, and I feel it puts you at risk for more heartache than it would if your father was around. Maybe if he was around, I would have picked better guys, or I wouldn't have gone back to those abusers, or maybe not even have been a teen mom; who really knows. What I do know is that you're never too old to want and need your father in your life. I didn't have that, and I can't say I wish I didn't because I do.

A Man's Love

From what I can recall, my first example of a true man's love was my fraternal grandfather Phil. Although I only had eight years with my grandpop, he left a tremendous impact on my heart and my life. He was such a loving grandfather. I have so many great stories about my grandfather and lots of memories to hold onto forever. Calling me Ivory Luv, which is my first and middle name, was something he started. Everyone followed suit after, and here I am, publishing my first book under it. When I would go over to his house, we always walked around the corner to Youngs Deli to get my favorite drink Yoo-hoo and potato sticks.

Times when I called, he would ask, "Who is this?" and I would say, "If you don't know, you better ask somebody!"

So, when he called and I asked, "Who is this?" he would say what I said to him. I still remember the smell and look of his apartment: the large fish tank and even the furniture. I miss him so much. Often, I wish he was still alive to be here for me. Especially to meet my children. I just know they would love him as much as I do. He would have been a great benefit in their lives.

Today, I tell them stories about him, and we look at the few pictures I have of us together. My grandfather was the first man to love me unconditionally, never break promises, and do just as he said he would for me. Although I know it wasn't his intention, it shattered my heart when he passed.

Even today, thinking back, I remember him lying in his casket and my uncle telling me to remember he loves me. My heart still aches. That was my favorite man in the whole wide world. I know that God doesn't make any mistakes, however. I love you, Grandpop; I'll forever hold on to your memories and share our stories. I hope you're proud of me. It has been an honor to be your Granddaughter.

The Second man to show me true man's love is my Uncle Billy. What I remember most about Uncle Billy is the father-like role model he was to me. He was more than an uncle by far. Everything I wanted in a father I had in him. Long talks, shopping trips, quality time, I could go on and on.

I remember him taking me late at night to clothing and shoe stores to prepare for my Disney trip the next day with my grandmother and aunt (his mother and sister). He bought me a few DKNY outfits, belts to match, and two pairs of hush puppies shoes. Every time my father promised me something and didn't follow through, there was my uncle coming to the rescue. One thing is this Disney character's two-sided pillow. I wanted the Beauty and the Beast one, and he got it for me—other things like jewelry and summer clothes.

More importantly, he always picked me up for days out, just him and I, sometimes my sister, came with. However, I was only eight and didn't understand much. On the day of my grandfather Phil's funeral (his father), I asked a bunch of questions. I guess no one knew how to answer them, really. He signaled for me to come down the row to him, sat me on his lap, and explained to me that my grandfather was no longer here with us. I still didn't understand; he just assured me that he would be okay and to remember the love that my grandfather and I shared.

He asked me if I knew how much my grandfather loved me, and I told him, "Yes." He said always remember that. He knew that I was sad, so he changed the subject. He was asking me if I liked Mickey Mouse because I had on Mickey Mouse jewelry. Uncle Billy told me he would get it cleaned and have diamonds put in the mouth of my Mickey ring. We smiled a little, and he hugged me.

One day on Halloween, I was getting ready to trick or treating, all dressed up as a tap dancer since I loved dancing so much. There was a knock at the door. My mother answered and told me it was for me. I went to the door with a huge smile and open arms. I loved visits from Uncle Billy.

He said, "Hey, Ivory Luv," and told me to say trick or treat. So, I did, and after I did, he put a $100 bill in my bag. I wanted candy, but he told me to buy my own but don't spend it all at once. Whenever my girlfriends and I were stuck somewhere, or I needed to go somewhere, I called Uncle Billy, and he came no hesitation. These memories are only a few; there were many more. Uncle Billy was a second father, and this is whom I looked up to as an example of a father.

The love of a man I have experienced more recently (well as an adult love) has been that of my husband. I have loved my husband since we met at the age of 14. Now don't get me wrong, I've been in some relationships and loved people, but it was nothing like this. What my husband shows me and has taught me is intentional love.

Although we have known each other for a very long time (21 years), coming back and rekindling our friendship in December 2015 was the best thing that could have happened to me. We always came back to one another and stayed in contact on and off since 2003, but since 2015, there has been steady contact and intentional investment at the right time.

He has always loved me and I him, but this time around, he showed me why I should be loved, what I deserved, and what love looks like. Also, it feels to be in love with someone and for someone to be in love with me, no strings attached. He gave me a different outlook on love and being with a man who loved me for me. He saw me when I didn't know what seeing myself was and loved me when I didn't know how to love myself. He adds on to what my grandpop and uncle have given me in my younger years, and it's so much to carry me through. I couldn't have asked for a better intentional forever love.

Big Ol'e Trash Bag

Many times, I thought about asking to move with my mother. The times when I was verbally abused or smacked because my sister and I were fighting. Other times it was because I couldn't wear what my uncle had bought me. My grandmother took the things my uncle bought me. She said that I didn't deserve them, even though they were mine!

By the time I was 14 and at the end of my freshman year of high school, I had had enough. I called my mom to ask if I could move with her. She asked me a bunch of questions, including why. I just told her I didn't want to be there anymore and was tired of getting in trouble for nothing all the time. She tried to convince me to stay until that school year was over. But there was no way no how I was staying any longer.

I asked and pleaded, "Please, Mom, let me go now instead of later."

She told me she would come down and talk to both of us. I told her my grandmother wouldn't admit anything and that I just wanted to move. I started packing my things up anyway. My grandmother didn't even know I was preparing to leave.

My mother came down and said, "Ivory wants to live with me." After talking to us, I guess she just gave in and told me to get my things. My Great-Aunt/God Mom was there and kind of witnessed some things and mediated. All my things were already packed in one *big ole black trash bag*. Everything I owned, clothes, shoes, and whatever else I had. Everything fit into that one bag. I dragged it down the steps and out the door. I didn't even say bye to my grandmother that day. I sat in that front seat and looked forward. I felt like I was getting a new start; I couldn't believe I was finally leaving!

When we first got to my mom's house, it was just me, my mom, my younger sister, and my younger brother there. My mother's husband wasn't there yet. I remember walking into my mother's house and smelling her favorite candle she had burning. I breathed a silent sigh of relief – I was home, a new start.

My mother always kept a clean house; I think that's where I get it from. My younger brother grabbed my bag and took it to my room. I didn't have my room at my grandmother's, and at my mother's house, I didn't have my own room either, but I didn't care. I just wanted a fresh start. My mother showed me where to put my clothes and told me to unpack them.

She told me dinner would be done in a little while. I just put my clothes away and sat in my room. My mother didn't dig deep into what was going on at my grandmother's. She never asked me how I was mistreated, but I didn't dwell on that too much. I was just happy I wouldn't have to deal with it anymore.

It was cool at my mom's. She went to work, and I went to school. She would pick me up after school almost every day, which was pretty cool. We came home each day. She went into her room, and we went into ours. I helped my siblings with their homework occasionally and did my stepsister's hair sometimes as well.

We sat on Sundays to eat Sunday dinner together. That's the only time my mother's husband sat with us and was home all day, so it felt good to sit as a family and eat dinner. I looked at my mom's house as a way out, but looking back, damn, I really had to beg my mother to move with her, yet my step-siblings had been living with her for years before I did. It felt horrible that my mother was raising someone else's children, but I was being raised by my grandmother and going through what I did there. A lot of the time, it made me angry at my mom. I was a child. I had no clue why, but I felt abandoned at those times.

I asked my mother recently why I didn't live with her as a child and asked if she knew what was happening in my grandmother's home. She said she didn't know what was going on, and if she knew sooner, I would have been with her. She told me she worked, and when we were younger, my grandmother told her to work and get herself together, and she'll take us in.

A little while later, she met her ex-husband, and because of his lifestyle at the time, she didn't want us in the house living with her. For years I blamed my step-siblings, and I didn't care how I treated them. I was mean to my stepsister, yes, she did aggravating things and knew how to get under my skin because she was living with our mom, but I was older, and I could have acted a little better. Things today I realize were absolutely wrong. They are only a few years younger than I am. I was only angry because they had my mother for years, and I felt like I didn't. I was hurt. I did, though, apologize as I got older with my actions and realized my sister was just a kid and couldn't have known what I felt or even understood it. My brother and I are really tight. We have a good relationship, and he was always silly and making me laugh. Our relationship, no matter what I felt, didn't suffer.

A few good memories I remember from when I used to stay the weekends at my mother's house before moving with her were the times we had family cookouts, and everyone came over to have a great time. My siblings and cousins even went to the WOW skating rink together, which is now called Rolling Thunder. We went to a late night jam session.

We loved to dance, so that was lots of fun. Another great time was the snowstorm of 03'. All of us siblings were snowed in together. The boys shoveled pavements and earned money. We found other things to do in the house. My mother had a finished basement which was set up like a family room, so we watched movies down there. We popped popcorn, made cocoa, and had a variety of chips and pretzels. We played board games; two of our favorites were

Sorry and Monopoly. We had a blast the times we got together at my mom's. Getting together with my siblings was a great time. Being at my mom's for good was even better.

Health

No one ever chooses to be a person with health issues. Someone who goes through countless surgeries, appointments, injections, medications, hospital stays, and everything else that comes with being a chronic illness warrior. Especially not at a young age. Having to go to sleep one day "regular" and then wake up to the start of what would be feeling like you're trapped in a different body that's not yours. This is just a little timeline of when my not-so-normal life started.

My health has been on a rocky, up-and-down path for some years now. I've had 17 surgeries since 2003, but I would like to say the trauma and consistency of surgeries started around 2008. I sprained my ankle three times back-to-back and hurt my knee in the process of one of those sprains in 2008. My knee never healed, even after my ankle sprain. I went on to get my knee looked at and found out I had a meniscus tear and lots of scar tissue buildup. And this was my first major surgery.

But let's start from the beginning. The first one, in 2003, was a gangling cyst removal on my left hand. It was too painful and huge for them to drain it, so they had to remove it. In 2006, I had to have all four of my wisdom teeth extracted. They were coming in sideways, causing swelling and pain in my face and throat. Next, I had a meniscus repair done to my right knee in 2011 from the trauma of my falling in 2008.

While going through therapy for my knee, my therapist sent me back to my orthopedic surgeon. I was experiencing some "popping and clicking" sounds and pain in my hips, specifically the right hip.

My knee doctor referred me to one of his colleagues who specialized in hips. While attending my appointment, I found out that I had a bone disease called Hip Dysplasia. This news was shocking! They told me I had to have this condition from birth because of how badly the hip ball and sockets were, but I was unaware of it until now. My parents didn't know anything about it either. He informed me that I needed to get surgery on my right hip immediately since it was the worst one.

So, in 2012, he performed an arthroscopy of the right hip to repair the labrum that was torn and shaved down some bone. It was supposed to be an outpatient surgery, but they ended up keeping me. My surgery went longer than expected because of how damaged my hip bone was when they went in to try and give me a better quality of life, and it caused a lot of pain afterward.

This was the first time I had to use a walker in my life to help me walk. I did PT and OT after being discharged, but none of that helped. In 2014, I went to get a second opinion because my hip wasn't healing, and I was in even more pain than I started out.

This new doctor wanted to get a Bilateral Periacetabular Osteoplasty (PAO) done. The recovery from this surgery was brutal. I had to learn how to walk again; I had a nurse and home health aide in the home three days a week, an occupational therapist, and a physical therapist three times a week as well. This was when I noticed I was depressed the most. I had to be washed up by my home health aide; I needed help doing everything. I medicated, slept, and mainly ate.

I eventually got moving. I even started a part-time job, trying to push myself a little more. My hips held up well for a few years, and then they started to feel like they were getting worse than before. I guess my body was rejecting the surgery, or it wasn't enough to hold up my damaged hips because I had to go back and be re-evaluated.

I had my tonsils removed in October 2014. Very painful, might I add. I found out while healing from that surgery that I had Gastroparesis.

After my doctor told me that the nausea and vomiting were just from having a reaction to anesthesia, I knew that couldn't be true. I've had too many surgeries and never had that issue. I could not eat nor keep liquids down. I had many stomach pains and lost 13 pounds in two weeks. I then went to see a Digestive Disease specialist at Temple Hospital. That is when I was diagnosed with this disease, Gastroparesis.

There was no cure, so I had to make changes in my diet to help or try meds. The medicine wasn't promising, so I opted out of it in the beginning. The only thing I took was nausea meds like Zofran. Sometimes, I could only tolerate drinking liquids or even baby food when I could not tolerate regular food. It at least helped with not being dehydrated and needing a feeding tube. I later tried different medications and trials to help, and nothing. To this day, I still have flare-ups and still hoping for a cure one day.

So here we are now in July of 2016. I am now 28 years old. I was living in another state, working, and trying to go on and be "normal." The pain and swelling continued, and it got worse in my hips. There were days I could not even get out of bed or walk up the stairs. I went back to see my doctor, and he told me it was time to get hip replacements and that we will do one at a time, about a year apart. He informed me that my hips were now slipping out the socket and that the socket was so highly shallow.

He gave me a date to have surgery in three days. Mind you, I only came down for a checkup appointment; I had no clue they were as bad as he said and that he would schedule the surgery that day and that soon. I knew this surgery would be life-changing, and I don't think I processed that I was actually getting a hip replacement. This surgery was tough. I cried so much. It was again me learning to walk differently than before. I gained a spinal headache three days after surgery and had to be rushed back to the hospital.

They gave me a medicine cocktail for migraines and rushed fluids for two days. Don't forget I just had hip surgery, so them lifting me to take x-rays to make sure I didn't have an infection (they thought that could be the cause of my pain and headache originally); running to the bathroom because of the fluids (of course I didn't run anywhere), and the headache that literally took until I was discharged to go away, which was two days later. I went home to finish healing and started PT and OT to strengthen and heal. I did pretty well but never fully completed it.

I pushed myself as much as I could until my left hip went out. Not even a year out, my left hip had to be replaced in February 2017. I cried a lot, and I self-medicated a lot. (Of course, the PAO surgery started this depression, but I came out of it when I started working and moved) It caused me to have a really rough recovery. I barely wanted to move or get out of bed.

I fell into a dark space; I was tired of being cut on and unable to move at a young age.

A little way into my healing of the second hip replacement, my incision opened and caused a little infection. I went to the hospital, and I had to be treated for that as well. I swelled so bad I couldn't move. My back became weak and swollen. I made it worse by not moving as much. But all I wanted to do was lay there. Through all of this, I still had to care for my two children. After my incision healed, I went to therapy and strengthened as much as I could there. The rest was up to me.

After my hip surgeries, I started working again. I actually pushed myself to start working that May for my second total hip replacement, just three months out of the surgery. I was determined to get out of work and be "normal," but I was also doing fairly well. I was doing pretty well at work until my fingers started giving out on me. It started with my right thumb. It would lock in a downward position, and sometimes it wouldn't budge. Sometimes it just gave off pain and clicked in and out of place. I never said anything to anyone; I just taped it some days and tried to work through it. The work I was doing I needed my fingers; I was working in a hair salon.

One day it got really bad. It locked in the downward position and swelled badly. I went

61

to a hand orthopedic specialist to see about it. He evaluated it and confirmed that I had trigger finger.

I received an injection that didn't quite help and ended up back at the office and him telling me I needed surgery. There were three more trigger releases to follow. This in which was my middle finger in my right hand, my left ring finger, and then the ring finger of my right hand. While getting the ring finger of my right hand fixed, I had to get scar tissue removed from my middle finger incision because that incision opened up, and it healed with a lot of scar tissue. It started to cause stiffness and pain, so he removed it while I was under.

Between the trigger releases from 2017, I had another hip surgery in July 2019. This one was through Plastic Surgery. My hips were pulling, tender, and hard, the same thing my hand was doing when that scar tissue built up. They discovered I had a lot of scar tissue that hardened and needed to be removed. You see, during my second hip replacement, I caught an infection. The scar opened up, and you know the rest.

My right one stiffened on its own, so they fixed both during surgery. In therapy, we tried everything to loosen them up, from scar putty to cupping to lots of different exercises. We even tried kinesiology tape. I got that surgery done, and it went very well. Took a lot to recover because I got both hips done simultaneously, but I was more motivated to heal from this one. I went back to therapy and graduated this time. I was ecstatic! My hips felt so much better, better than they did before the first surgery in 2012. Very much long overdue, but this wasn't the end of my surgeries...

In 2020, I had bad breast pain. It was painful to lift my arms or even when I was at rest. I had back pain and neck pain as well. I was more comfortable in a sports bra than a regular wired bra. I went to see an Oncologist to evaluate this breast discomfort. I got a mammogram and ultrasound, and they found two lumps. They had to do a biopsy to test them.

I was scared and crushed by this news. The biopsies came back that one was benign, and the other was inconclusive and graded suspicious. When they grade something suspicious, it tells the patient they need to keep an eye on it because they are unsure what it is. They told me I had to return every six months to ensure it didn't grow.

I went through pain for a few months still and ended up making the appt a little sooner than six months. They found the lump grown and opted to remove both lumps to be safe. February 2021, I had bilateral mass excisions when they went in, they found three lumps instead of two. Recovery wasn't as bad as I thought it would be. The results came back they were benign. They still asked to follow up within the next year to make sure no more grew and the pain left.

Here I am in October 2022, and I am still having pain. I also have two more lumps, but they are very small. My oncologist sent me to a plastic surgeon because we both agreed that a reduction would most likely help. I have extremely dense and calcification breast tissue as well.

November 2022, I received my surgery. I had a mammoplasty (breast reduction) and was told that lots of nasty breast tissue was removed. They couldn't quite confirm that all fibroadenomas were removed because they were so small, but they believed they were.

After this surgery, my oxygen level kept dropping low, and my blood pressure as well, so I was in recovery a little longer than expected. I experienced some difficulty while healing. I somehow had two infections that caused me to need four different antibiotics, one of which I had a bad reaction. The healing took a little longer. Two parts of my right breast opened up, so that prolonged things. Nine months later and everything has healed great.

I was also diagnosed with Rheumatoid Disease, Psoriatic Disease in 2020, and Sjogren's Syndrome in October 2022.

These are all known as Autoimmune diseases. Your immune system is attacked in different ways. I have POTS (Dysautonomia), which got worse after I had Covid May 2022 and recently in December 2022 right before the new year, while healing from surgery. Having this diagnosis after having covid the first time caused me to be considered a long hauler of covid. It also caused a lot of my Rheumatologic symptoms to get worse during that time. Everything is being evaluated accordingly and being very well managed.

Yes, this was a lot to read. You're probably asking me how you are handling this. I am not sure myself. Honestly, I don't know if I'm coming or going some days. I'm unsure if it's just my body and what it needed to go through or if all of these contributed to my autoimmune disease that we didn't know about sooner. All of the flares constantly, hospital stays, kidney infections, and so much more.

Now being 35 years old, it's still very hard to fathom all that I've been through and going through. I tend to keep moving forward and stay stuck as much as possible, but I also don't give myself enough credit sometimes, but here and now, starting with this book, I will! If you are reading this and you have medical issues that you are fighting through, understand that you can get through them and continue to fight on.

In life, we never expect to be dealt certain types of hands, but I believe that everything happens for a reason or a season. This reason is to help you know you're not alone and that you now know a little bit of someone who is surviving the same thing or something similar to what you are going through, and I'm making it.

Family and Friends support your loved ones going through. We know you may be tired of hearing it or even seeing them go through, but can you imagine what they are going through? Can you imagine feeling trapped in a body you have no control over? Remember to have empathy, check in, and even just send a little text or call from time to time to let them know you're thinking about them and that they're not alone. Trust me, that would mean more than you would know.

One Day At

A Time

Addiction is something I never thought would be a part of my story. I never saw pain medication misuse as an addiction or even saw that I was even misusing opioids. I was on pain medication since my first surgery, which was my wisdom teeth removal. I was on Vicodin. That didn't seem to be an issue. I wouldn't say I liked the way they made me feel, so I didn't take them for long.

As surgeries and procedures continued, I was on all types of medications, Vicodin, Tylenol with codeine, dilaudid, tramadol, and even morphine. Yes, I know I had a lot of surgeries, but the issue came in when I didn't separate the need from the want. This problem started in about 2011.

I became dependent on opioids pretty fast. I suffered from up and down moods, and depression when stopping them abruptly. When you're depressed, you don't want to move. You want to forget about everything you ever went through and be alone. The pain also made me feel alone. I used opioids to make me numb and forget things.

I lost weight initially from the episode after my tonsillectomy, but the weight dropped more. Still, I didn't recognize that I had a problem.

I stopped Cold Turkey in 2015. I stopped taking them entirely without weaning off them. This is when I moved to a different state because I wanted a fresh start. I decided that I wasn't going to take opioids for illegitimate reasons. I wouldn't try to cover up the stress, depression, and hurt through self-medicating. I didn't realize it was called Cold Turkey. I didn't think I was abusing it; most people never do. I decided to start with a clear mind and new beginnings. That lasted for a good year or so until the surgeries started up again.

Losing my grandmother, watching her transition was a bit traumatizing. Self-medicating became worse for me again. Nobody knew. I've had so many surgeries that getting opioids was a norm, and it wasn't questioned, not yet, anyway. I remember my husband saying, "Maybe not take as much and see how you do."

I was still healing from surgery at that time and getting a little of my strength back. I was very defensive and extremely irritable with his statement. Deep down, I was defending this addiction. I didn't even recognize fully that I had, or maybe I didn't care.

I would go to the hospital more than I needed to get "quick fixes," as I like to refer to them. Intravenous opioids were always better than pills. It was terrible behavior, come to think about it. I'm sure I neglected the people that I love and even my children at some point. I know I never abused them or anything, but brushing them off and not giving them the attention they deserve is just as bad.

Years ago, I wouldn't have even realized I was doing these things, but who I am today, I understand those negative behaviors, and I'm learning from them. Maybe I can save someone else from doing these things or help bring awareness to a problem that's starting.

The first time I realized I had an issue was when I was sitting at a bus stop with my kids in 2018, and I believe I fell asleep because I felt myself nod. I had taken something before leaving to go to a friend's house. I had my children with me. I cried, and I ended up walking across the street to Dunkin Donuts to get coffee to try and keep me up to be present for my kids. I got to my friend's house and told her what happened.

I told her I needed to be done and stop because I believed them to have been a problem, then I told my husband. They both supported me and did not judge me. I went Cold Turkey again. This time it stuck, though, and it was hard.

About a month later, I was hospitalized for pneumonia and the flu. I always got sick, so it didn't cross my mind that I was going through withdrawal. I had many other things going on outside of that sickness too. I was on and off, depressed and crying; my stomach was in a lot of pain.

I didn't realize how unstable I was. I asked my husband one day later if he thought my being sick was me going through withdrawal, and he said that's exactly what it was. That he didn't want to scare me is why he had everyone coming to check on me while in the hospital. They didn't know why everything was happening, so they did a lot of tests; shoot, neither did I.

I was at one hospital for more than a week, and then they discharged me. I went home and wasn't feeling better. I was very swollen, weak, and fatigued, so I went to another hospital for a second opinion, and they kept me. My heart rate raised when I took a few steps, and so they wanted to run tests to make sure my heart was fine, and it was, so I was then discharged a week later. Looking back, that journey was pretty tough.

That first year was the toughest. Lots of mixed emotions, ups and downs, wanting to relapse, suicide ideologies, and many more things, but I made it through. My husband put together a one-year Soberversary surprise gathering, and it was pretty cool. I'm not sure I could take it all in, but for some reason, four years later, I am recognizing everything. I hear it's pretty normal for those first few years to be tough and that although it can become a struggle at any time, recognizing the gift of it and those celebrating you in these milestones is a blessing.

Today I am four years clean and serene, and by the time this publishes, I'm praying to be five years clean. For the rest of my life, I will be considered a recovering addict because no matter how many years clean you are, it is always something you must watch and fight through. Some days are harder than others. Be aware of your triggers and what sets you off. No matter how many days, months, or even years you have clean, I suggest taking every day like it's your first day, one day at a time.

When you know what your life is worth and how self-medicating will affect you and those around you, you know what to stay clean for and what staying clean would do for you and yours. You must remember that you must do it for YOU first and foremost. If you do it for anybody else, you will always run into back slides. Find a hobby or two. Get to a meeting often and find a sponsor. Try not to pick up another habit; it's easy to do this as well. I tend to read, write, exercise, or do activities with my children to keep them busy; it helps. Keep positive people around you, people who have your best interest at heart and who support you through your mistakes and help you get and stay on track of being sober.

I refuse to let any of my ailments stop me from succeeding and caring properly for my children and myself ever again. That's the mindset I love to keep permanently. Every day I get up and push to be a better me. Every day I pray for better health. There are some days when I don't want to move. We will all have those days but push past them and don't go back into bad behaviors; it only makes things worse, not better. What God has planned for me, I'll never know. Neither do you. Self-medicating is easy; take the not-so-easy road and fight the urges, push through, and stay positive. Depression attacks a weak and hungry mind; stay busy and active.

SIDEBAR: *Tramadol is always easily given, but it became my drug of choice. I honestly think this is the worse drug to be prescribed to anyone. If Tylenol and Ibuprofen don't work and they want to give you tramadol, please ask for something else. In the beginning, I did not realize how many I was taking. It's so addictive. In my honest opinion, it's worse than Percocet, Vicodin, and any high-class narcotic. I think this to be true because it doesn't give you the symptoms as the others, but it makes your body crave* *it even when you don't need it. So many people who have been prescribed this told me they were addicted to this as well. Everyone is different; just be mindful of this drug, please. Also, stay away from the other ones if you don't necessarily need them as well.*

The Importance Of Celebrating Your Accomplishments.

T his is something I had to learn over time. I never celebrated myself or my accomplishments. I always looked for someone else to celebrate me or the "Big win." I never gave myself any credit and was hard on myself more than anything. I was my worse critic, and yes, I know most times we are, but not at the expense of losing yourself in it. I didn't even recognize the people that did their best to celebrate me either because I didn't feel it myself.

If you constantly wait on others to celebrate you and you don't celebrate, your first one or two things will happen. You will either not appreciate those that do, or you will be waiting a lifetime. I believe my wanting to be celebrated came from the fact that I wasn't as a kid. I remember doing my very best because I wanted people to talk about me and praise me.

Sometimes they did, but not those that I wanted to see me. I did this all the way up until now. I stopped throwing myself parties, inviting people out to celebrate me, and doing all the planning to not be happy. Either it was forced, or people didn't show up. So, I was disappointed either way. This year I'm sitting in me; I'm sitting in, not putting myself out there or planning anything but seeing what I could do for myself. It didn't feel good at first, but I did it.

The first time I did it was on my 4-year Soberversary, Sept 19, 2022. Now I can't lie I was still sad that day. I cried a lot, especially because I was struggling with it at that time; on top of that, it still didn't feel good not to be celebrated by my loved ones. I was looking for someone to pick me up and validate me, and that wasn't happening.

After the tears and listening to my husband, I got up and took myself and the kids to dinner. I'm happy I did because I went to the same restaurant I always go to and this time my waiter happened to ask me if I was there to celebrate anything. I told him what I was celebrating, and he made that evening so special.

He had a dessert specially made for me with "Congrats" written on the plate. So simple, yet he made my night. On top of that, he had a card signed by all the staff there. Some even put words of encouragement on the card. To think, I was going to stay home that night and not even celebrate myself.

He told me that he had a few friends that are also in recovery, and he just wanted to honor my four years that night. It warmed me, and I cried but this time grateful tears. My reason for telling this little story is that you never know what blessings will come your way by putting yourself first and celebrating yourself. Celebrate yourself because you are in charge of your dopamine.

Anything you get from anyone else is extra, and whatever they don't give you won't be missed. Appreciate and celebrate you first. Your accomplishments are something you work hard for, and a lot of times, the people around you can't see your hard work. Rather it's because they don't want to, or they are silently missed. You are all the happiness you need, and if you worked hard or got to where you are, why not celebrate the person who did it?

As Catherine Pulsifer said,
"Accomplishments give you a sense of confidence and encouragement."

Mental Health

Mental health plays such a big role in my life. It plays a big role because that's part of where I get my strength from. In 2019 I was diagnosed with Manic Depressive Disorder, PTSD, and Anxiety. Manic depression is also known as bipolar disorder.

For example, you might feel anxious when faced with a difficult problem at work, before taking a test, or before making an important decision. It can help you to cope. The anxiety may give you a boost of energy or help you focus. But for people with anxiety disorders, the fear is not temporary and can be overwhelming.

I knew for years something was not all the way together with me, but let me explain.

I've been through a lot, as you have read thus far, but I never talked to anyone professional about it, and I acted out because of it. I cried a lot. Crying is good when you're not drowning in your tears. I would cry until I was sick. Not purposefully, but that's how much and how bad I cried.

I remember crying for three days straight on many occasions. The first time this happened, my doctor referred me to a therapist, who then referred me to a psychiatrist. In 2011, He diagnosed me with depression. He put me on a medication that made me feel like a zombie, which I didn't like. I stopped the medicine because I could not function doing day-to-day tasks. I never went back to therapy, and I picked up opioids and alcohol shortly after.

Later down the line, my second one was after my hip surgery, but I still had opioids and alcohol. That only patched up feelings or numbed me for the moment. In 2019, I spent days crying on and off, stayed in my room, didn't eat, slept a lot, and was snappy. Then there were other times I was so motivated up and moving that I had insomnia, a lot of energy, and then I crashed.

This was my cycle, and I noticed it more because I didn't have opioids and alcohol to numb those feelings anymore. But let's go back even further before I move forward to actually being diagnosed and how that came about.

Early on, I dealt with pain-inflicting and suicide ideologies. The first time I thought of ending my life, I was nine years old. I tried to hurt myself by digging into my wrist with a safety pin, a really big thick one. Although, that's not what I originally wanted to use. It was math class, and I was in the fourth grade at Elmwood Middle School. With all the issues and unhappiness at home and the bullying at school, I didn't feel the need to be around anymore. Nobody would miss me anyway, was my thinking.

My plan was I would go home, get a knife from the kitchen and slit my wrists in my room. For the rest of the day, I planned how I would do it in my head and replayed it repeatedly. These thoughts put me at ease, and all the bullying that went on that day didn't bother me one bit because I knew it would be all over soon.

For as long as I can remember, I was bullied. Either it was because I was smart, I wasn't cool enough, I was the new girl, or even for having long hair. Trying to fit in with everybody got me into trouble. I would talk in class, or get smart, just so the girls could laugh and like me. That didn't work. They still teased me and pushed me around. It happened until I fought back in high school.

Okay, back to fourth grade. Once I got home from school, I looked and realized my plan had to be switched somehow. My grandmother was in the kitchen cooking, so that I couldn't get a knife. Once I realized that, I went upstairs to come up with another plan. I went into my room to think; then it hit me! I went to her room and hesitated at the door. Just then, my thoughts were confirmed; everything came to mind about why I wanted to do it.

I walked into her room which always smelled like Avon Products, Skin-so-soft, to be exact, I looked for something, and I came across a big thick safety pin. The safety pin was on the corner of her dresser. I remember digging and scratching until I became numb to the pain and comfortable.

At first, it was painful, not as painful as the pain I felt through the abuse and bullying, though. To be bullied every day and then go home and not be happy was so not ideal. At home, I was also teased. I was called names, and I was sad a lot.

Fear was nowhere in my mind at this point; I was just ready to be at peace: no more pain, No more crying, No more mistreatment. There was blood, but not enough to bleed out. It was the only object that I could find. So, I just cut with the safety pin to get relief. That's what I got from that. I got tired and eventually went to sleep. From that day, the pain inflictions started. I did it often from time to time, even in adulthood.

At the age of 14, I had thoughts to end my life again. There were a pair of purple scissors that I took. I dug and cut at the same areas I did a few years prior. I also cut a spot in between my thumb and pointer finger; that cut was deep, and I saw the most blood come from that part.

There was a sense of relief that came upon me, and I was happy. I thought, finally, this could be it. Just when I went to cut more, I was called downstairs. I had to hurry and clean up the blood as much as I could. I knew if my grandmom saw it, she would ask, and I wanted it to happen silently.

I got a Band-Aid and put it where the deepest cut was and put something on my arms to hide the cuts as well. A jacket or a long sleeve shirt, I can't really remember which one it was. The cut was bleeding a lot too. I went downstairs, and there was mail for me. I was asked about the bleeding because it was showing through the Band-Aid. I said the scissors cut me by accident while looking for something in the drawer, but that wasn't the case at all.

My grandmother told me not to go back in there, and that was that. The letter was from a program. I had been accepted into The Young Scholars Program. This made me feel I would have a little freedom, and just maybe I did mean something in this world. Those thoughts didn't all the way go away, but they were suppressed some. With this program, I would be out of the house every day; I met friends, I laughed and danced. Although I had to go back home after, that little escape felt like fresh air.

About 17 years later, I self-inflicted again. I'm sure it was times in-between as well because I also punched walls, but honestly, I don't remember everything that happened at the height of my taking all the opioids. It was at another rough time. I had a huge argument with my mom.

We bumped heads a lot, and I was living with her at the time. It was terrible and I was already angry, healing from surgery, and just in a bad spot. I had just moved back to her house and felt like I lost everything, even myself. I cut over my tattoo where her name was. I punched the wall that day as well. All of it was a temporary anger release yet later caused damage (hint, my hand surgeries).

So now we fast forward to my diagnoses and how they came about. I was encouraged to seek therapy and a psychiatrist because I was in another place of feeling like I didn't belong there. I called and went right away. I had an immediate appointment with my psychiatrist, and we did an evaluation.

She didn't ask me about anyone in my family, and if they were diagnosed with anything, she just focused on me. So, we finished this evaluation, and it was determined that I was manic-depressive; I suffered from PTSD and anxiety. She also explained that the medication I was given years ago made me like that because it was not treating both sides of my disorder. I can't lie.

When I first received these diagnoses, I was bummed. I didn't want to be so "different." I thought this would be why people would use it against me or look at me differently. I eventually accepted it. I'm glad I did because I saw a change in me for the better. I am on medication that works for me, and it helps me function. I'm not so up and down, and I'm not all over the place. I can focus and complete tasks. I can help my son through his mental health, and I have been a great example to and for him and that I am proud of. I have these diagnoses; these diagnoses don't have a hold on me.

Nancy and Sig

These two people, Nancy and Sig, helped
me to know that I have always had a
purpose in life. They reminded me of
how smart I was and how I could achieve
anything I wanted to do and be in life. The way
they came into my life was nothing short of
God's work.

My grandmother wrote to Operation
Santa Claus when I was 9 or 10. This was a
program that helped bring gifts and clothes to
needy families. I didn't know about it when I
was younger, but I learned about the program
as I grew up. Nancy and Sig were our family's
donators. I'm not too sure about how it works,
but that's how we met them. They came in one
night with gifts for Christmas and asked to meet
us.

Most Operation Santa Claus donators don't meet the children; they just donate. They were different, though. They offered to help us in many ways. They tutored us in whatever subject we struggled in. They were so patient, nice, and understanding. I also remember when I first got my menstrual cycle, Nancy came and bought me a book. It was called "Are you there God? It's Me Margaret" by Judy Blume. Also, other books she knew would help me in life. I had no clue about anything, but the books helped me.

My older brother, younger sister, and I also stayed over at their house on some Thanksgiving nights or even the day after and helped them prepare dinner. We tried new foods, and we always enjoyed root beer floats and popcorn at night. I make my mac and cheese the way Nancy showed us, with breadcrumbs on top. I love baked squash because of them, and I know what it means to appreciate the small things around the holidays because of Nancy and Sig.

I lost contact with them after moving with my mother, and I just didn't want anything connected to where I used to live. My brother always encouraged me to call them. I felt like I couldn't because there was such a gap in communication over the years. I felt that I let them down with how I didn't go to college and be the best they always told me I could be. I always intended to reach out one day and just let them know how much they've helped me and been a big part of my life. I know they'll be extremely proud of me once they see me now.

Although when I saw them at my brother's wedding in 2012, they told me to never stop reaching for my goals. They told me how much they were still proud of me and how smart I was. I love them for keeping confidence instilled in me. Their voices will always be in my head. Also, how much motivation they gave me in my early years. I was blessed with them being around, and I'm blessed to have met them.

Trauma

Trauma has a way of showing up at times; you have no clue they would. It's so many times I was triggered or am triggered, and I couldn't understand why. A lot of the times, I didn't know I was traumatized. I always thought that trauma came from things like war and heavy things in life. I didn't identify my childhood issues, abuse, or even my addiction as trauma, but let's look at the definition of trauma.

So, you see, trauma can literally come after anything in our lives, and it kind of surrounds me with my PTSD diagnosis. My therapist described it as being your brain's way of thinking you're going to be retraumatized again; it gives you anxiety for you to fight your way out of it. Even if it isn't a situation, you actually need to fight. It's automatically your brain telling you to go into flight mode. He said it's called a maladaptive mechanism.

What that basically is, your coping generally increases stress and anxiety, with examples such as self-harm, escape, intrusive thoughts, procrastination, binge eating, or even substance abuse. The more this behavior continues, it puts you at risk of continuing these harmful behaviors or even making them work.

Maladaptive coping is also unhealthy. It holds us back from our full potential and causes harm in positive situations and relationships. They may even prevent us from socializing and lead us to isolation. That's what it did to me a lot. I would cancel plans last minute and isolate. This was unhealthy, but it seemed the only solution to my brain's madness. You can, however, replace those negative traits with more productive ones. I was talking about them to a therapist and healing from them, finding a hobby, or even forgiving the people who have hurt me.

Therapy always seems to be my go-to when talking to someone who has these traits as well. We can't heal on our own, and many times, when we try to do it with loved ones, it ends up hurting them or being too much for them. Understand that the first therapist that you sit with may not be for you. Shop around and find someone you're comfortable with and be consistent with your sessions. That's my advice.

Therapy doesn't always work for everyone, and there are different ways to heal. Some do it in the form of writing (hint: me), some through dance, some through art, some through praying solely, and some even through music. Find something that will help you break down these traits and work on them one day at a time; if I can do it, so can you!

Don't forget that I'm still doing the work every single day, and some days are harder than others. Sometimes my resources help those hard days, and sometimes they don't, and that day is a bad day, but I know I'll always have tomorrow. When taking it day by day gets tough, take it hour by hour.

What Is Love?

Love comes in different ways. There's parental love, family love, spousal/mate love; there's love you have for your children, self-love, love of and for money; there's the love you have for something you're passionate about and want to be in life, etc. All of which could leave you with a broken heart at some point in time in your life. I want to say that through broken hearts, there are always lessons to be learned.

Only you will understand and notice those lessons when you want to notice them. Rather it's learning to choose a better mate, to make better financial decisions, or learning to treat your family and friends better and not take them for granted or setting boundaries for how you want them to treat you; a lesson is a lesson.

Sometimes we don't learn that broken-hearted lesson the first time and tend to make that mistake that leaves us brokenhearted repeatedly. Eventually, though, that lesson is learned and applied to some of us. We make better decisions to avoid the outcome we experienced in previous decisions.

Love helps us grow and grow up. I was awarded a large sum of money which I spent on other people instead of something beneficial to me, which woke me up. When I had children, that woke me up. When I lost my grandmother, that woke me up. When I went through domestic violence, and being negatively used by my partners, that woke me up; it took the love and loss of things to wake me up; as you can see, everything didn't always stick. Today I see a little clearer; notice I said a little. I can't say I see all the way clear because I don't quite know everything there is to know in life. So, I say a little clearer.

I have, most importantly, learned to love myself first. As I learn to do that, I am learning to understand what part I play in everything that happened to me. Also, where I went wrong in loving the things and people I did or thinking it was love anyway. Setting standards and boundaries for myself and others also plays a big part.

Loving myself first helps me to be headstrong and think clearer when making decisions. Not just acting but thinking about it first and then deciding. With that, I've learned better management skills with money; I've learned what true and real love is with my children Nyiem and Zaynah and through the love of my Husband. I have learned to let others love me. I am now able to distinguish what real love is and who doesn't and doesn't love me. Most importantly, I've learned the love of God. When you don't love yourself, you can't really see the love God has for you. That's why you question and don't appreciate Him, especially when you're going through it. I've learned that God loves me, and He places people in your life that love you for reasons and seasons.

The love my children show me is indescribable. They have shown me what true love really is. How to love someone so innocent and precious and how to be gentle as well. That's a different kind of love from a family or mate's love.

Do not give up on love. Don't give up the love of your passion, even if you keep failing and nothing seems right. Keep loving it and pushing forward. It's coming. Don't give up on the love of family; they may not see things your way or even support you at times but understand that they still may love you, and it's okay to love them, even with differing opinions. It's also okay to build your own little family and love them unconditionally, intentionally.

Never ever give up on the love of your children. No matter what you're struggling with. No matter what they may be doing or what you have going on. Understand that when you go through, they go through with you. So be patient. Understand that there is unconditional love out there. Love yourself fully! That's the first step of even loving anyone else.

Don't give up on finding love and being in love. I believe there's truly someone out there for everyone. I never knew mine was in my life all along. I don't regret anything I've been through because I've learned a lot. I honestly don't believe that we would be together had I never gone through the things I did. I wouldn't have been able to see my husband as clearly as I do today. I probably wouldn't have let him in.

Be thankful for your past. Your mistakes, your bad decisions, and the experience and understanding you've gained from all. I know that everything surely happens for a reason. Through trusting God's plan and not my own, I see things so much clearer, and I love that much more. Please don't give up on love, everyone needs it, and everyone deserves it. YOU deserve it!

Self-Love is something I often talk about at my events and gatherings. I'm always stressing the importance of loving yourself and knowing how to love yourself properly so that someone else knows how to. You have to treat yourself with the same expectation that you hold everyone else to. People often feed off how you treat yourself.

Loving on you includes but is not limited to treating yourself to some of your favorite scents and items, running yourself a bubble bath and lighting candles and relaxing, or even something simple as sitting quietly by yourself and giving yourself full permission to be in you. If that means saying no to protect your mental health so that you can love yourself, then do that. Self-Love also ties into your health, your mental and your physical. Making sure you're healthy and making healthy decisions.

Self-Neglect is neglecting what's important to you and for you. You lose care for yourself, and you don't put what is essential to you FIRST! We have to stop looking for others to build the love in us. We should always understand that anything anyone else gives us is extra love and care. Self-Love is not letting us feel down on ourselves; setting those boundaries and standards with ourselves is needed too.

We should love ourselves the best way we know how and learn ways to do so if we don't. Here are some things I do for myself: write, take soothing bubble baths, put on cute PJs and lay on real rose petals, buy myself flowers, permit myself to cry, and buy things that make me feel loved. Don't think that you're not loving yourself because you're not doing everything loving to yourself. Don't let it be the end all be all.

I, too, have things I'm not quite good with, like giving myself enough credit, telling myself it's okay to feel down some days and still grieve, and yelling when I'm angry or not realizing I have leveled up. Even if it's the most minor thing, I tend to overlook it. Are these things loving to me? No, of course not. Can these things be fixed and changed? Of course, they can, and I'm working daily to do that and staying in the now and loving myself more than neglecting myself.

Loving me precisely at the expectation that I want someone to love me and building positive affirmations. We are capable of great things in our life. Thank yourself and celebrate your accomplishments. Let go of negative comparisons. You don't have to live up to what the world says you should be. Be exactly who you want to be and feel like you're born to be, starting with self-love.

Relationships

R elationships can be hard. As long as you push for them and set boundaries and standards, things will be good. I know I've been mentioning boundaries, and it means a lot, and I promise we'll get into that next. I've always struggled with relationships. Either it was me picking the wrong people to invest in, putting my all into them to the point I had nothing left for myself, expecting people to give me what I've been giving them, wanting to make everybody a priority over me, and then being mad about it, expending myself into other people's problems and using more sympathy than empathy.

Sympathy is when you drown yourself in the person's problem and get too emotionally attached, whereas, with empathy, you understand what they're going through; you help problem solve the problem and give tools or resources to help. Making sure you separate the two or even just not entirely have sympathy to the point that it affects your well-being and who you are also growing to be.

You also have to remember not to prioritize everyone the same. Sometimes we put people in groups where they simply don't belong. If someone is there for a specific reason, don't cross the line of making them more than that. This goes for romantic, family, or even friendships. Let me explain deeper.

I had a conversation with one of my older cousins as I was in a storm of not understanding what was happening in my life and not understanding why relationships kept falling out or apart. Let me share what she told me because it helped me a lot.

She told me everybody has three circles of people in their life. We should only really have two, but sometimes we hold on to that last circle, too, as if we'll be missing something. Have you ever been confused about who people are to you and what place they belong in your life? This is where the Three Circles come into play. Your life will revolve around these three circles. Once I explain them, you will begin to place people in the circles (silently). I guarantee your life would start to be a little easier with grouping the people in your life into these categories.

The first circle is the best circle for me. Let's call this circle "Main Ones." Within this circle, there should only be about one or two people in this circle, maybe three tops. This doesn't have to be what the world says it "should" be. It doesn't have to be someone you have known for 10+ years, your momma, your cousin, or even your sister. Sometimes it's your neighbor, brother, or even someone you met two years ago.

In this circle, these people have your back. They never let you down. You may only talk some of the time, but when you need them for whatever and they have the means to do it or give it, they do.

Most of the time they will even find a way to get it done for you. They know all your secrets; you trust they would never spread or tell anyone else. They always enjoy hearing your issues, and they give you the best advice in all situations. They don't hate on anything you have going on. They are your best friends, Your ride or die's, down for whatever... your Main Ones!

The second circle is a comfortable circle. This circle is called "Use what we can." Using someone is not bad when it's done right. In this circle, you give and take. This circle is for when you carpool, when you want to go to a concert when you want to go to lunch, and so forth. So, you see, this group is your friends and family; however, you don't tell this group all your business.

You keep this group real general. Don't confuse this group with your "Main Ones" because sometimes we do so. Sometimes we slip and make someone in this group a "Main One" and wonder why we're being shitted on. Most of the time, it's our fault because we let them get there and put them in a place they do not belong. Check yourself, check your group because that isn't it.

The third and final circle isn't healthy. Let's call this circle straight what it is the "Ain't sh*t" circle." This circle drains you, and nobody should literally be here that you talk to unless you want to get burned. These people take and take and take but don't give you shit. No, I'm lying. They give you little sometimes to keep you hanging on...if you let them. They give you just what you need to make you stay around or think they are in your life for the long haul. They take until you have nothing, not even energy. If you let them, they will drain you dry of everything. They give bad advice, and they root for your failure.

The one time you can't do for them, it's the end of the world. They may say, "Oh, that's okay," but you better believe they're either going to act funny or "keep that same energy" with you like you meant not to be there or do what they're asking on purpose. They really can give two shits about you besides what they can get from you. Stay away from these selfish people. They can be whoever is around you. They may be your family or friends you have known for years. Let them go no matter who they are and what "title" they may have.

Now you see how important these circles are. How they can better your life and help you to maneuver in this world, we call life. How can you best choose your relationship with people and set those boundaries for yourself with those you love and those who no longer need to be in your life? Make this decision based on facts.

Even if you must make a list and weigh your good and bad about that person, do it. This also helps to categorize where people stand in these circles and your life. Hold yourself accountable for your actions and decisions in the process of this decision-making. Anything you allow is ultimately up to you.

I don't want to leave out that you must always appreciate your relationships and be intentional with them. Love your people and treat them with the same love and respect that you want them to with you.

Don't take for granted the people in your life and those who are there for you, good and bad. Relationships do go through hiccups, but what matters most is that both parties actively work to make things better. We grow every day, so we must learn to grow through our relationships and accept new things and where they grow to go. Whether they stay in the circles, they are in or fall off. Here's another analogy. Relationships can also be classified as a tree in its seasons.

First, we'll start with the Leaves. The wind blows this and that way, moving the leaves around, making them unstable. They fall off, crumble, and turn colors. The season changes; they wither and die, then they're gone. Most people in the world are like that; they're just there to take and give shade now and then, nothing more, nothing less. Leave these people where they are and take them for what they show you to be.

You can't save them. Sorry, not Sorry. Next are the branches. Be careful with the branches. They will fool you. They will make you think they are strong support and sturdy, but as soon as you step on them or pull too hard, they will break.

Be careful what you tell these types of people and how much you give them access to your life; they aren't stable supporters. Lastly, we have the Roots. Roots are grounded! Roots are the main source of the tree. You are the first root. They ride for you and are not going anywhere. They don't care to be seen; they don't care for people to know they do things for you or tend to be acknowledged for it. Of course, you should, but they don't do it for any of that, so it doesn't bother them.

It's only a few roots on a tree compared to the branches and leaves. Treat your roots right because, remember, to have branches and leaves; you need those roots as a foundation. If you tell someone they're hurting, you and you see them actively trying to fix it, keep them around; that's a leaf trying to grow into something else and better your relationship with them or even a branch.

Now if you tell someone they hurt you, and they flip on you and keep doing it, they don't care. Get rid of them and move on, no matter how much it hurts. It will get easier as the days go on.

Boundaries / Standards

Setting boundaries and standards is important for all relationships. It helps expectations, the dynamic of the relationship, and also communication. It's not always easy, and things will change as you see fit in every relationship. You won't always have the same boundaries for every relationship; however, your standards may be the same with a little twist.

A boundary is a line that marks the limits of an area, a dividing line. A standard is a minimum requirement, a level of quality or attainment. To me, it's a basis on what you allow and won't allow. Sometimes we tell our loved ones what they are; sometimes, we'll keep that mental note or write it down for ourselves. They're not just for everyone else in your life, but they're also for you, actually for you first.

113

These have allowed me not to drain myself dry and not to get so involved when need be.

Setting boundaries help you to know what you will and won't tolerate. Boundaries are put in place to keep your self-love whole, and they help you from being used. It allows you to be respected and for you to respect yourself. Whatever those are, stand on them. Now don't get me wrong, sometimes you bend them. Something you won't be willing to tolerate with your man you don't mind with your girlfriends. Or something you don't watch when you and your partner are good; it simply can't be said or done when y'all are not good. Everything should have a balance.

Also, don't expect people to live by your boundaries if you don't tell them what they are; however, it is still your choice to do so. I find it easier to say to them so that they know what you like and don't like, what you'll tolerate and won't tolerate. Setting boundaries and drawing a line is healthy as long as you're willing to hold people and yourself to them.

For instance, if I set a boundary of not being cussed at, but I don't say I don't really mind if we're swearing while we're good and holding a conversation, it may come up later. If you argue and curse words fly, then it's "Don't curse at me. You know I don't like that", whereas they could follow and say when, "We were good. You didn't have an issue with it."

So be clear about them. You can also set a consequence. No, not like you're a child, but you know to let that person know you're serious about that boundary. You don't have to be harsh or mean about it, but I believe clear communication is best with boundaries.

Standards are just about the same. To me, they go hand and hand. Standards are more general; for instance, you may want to be respected by all and not belittled. You may want your mate to have a job, no kids, a 5-year goal, your own place, etc. It's just things you want the people in your life to have or respect about you. Things you won't really color outside the lines for. They are things a person may have before the next level with you or even before meeting you at that first level. Standards are more than likely never change or are something that can't be persuaded to change. I call it your fairytale yet realistic goals.

In all, boundaries and standards are lifelong lines for those in your life, especially your love life, that can't be crossed and have to be respected in order to function with who you are. Be consistent with your boundaries and standards. Anything that you allow to happen to you is ultimately on you without boundaries put in place. With your standards, don't be afraid to bend a little; there may be potential in a person with a dream, but be smart! Protect who you are and what you will not allow from others.

Growth:

The Process Of It All

G rowth comes when you are willing to admit your faults and get uncomfortable with where you are. Knowing that you want to change is just the first part of it. That's where I started anyway; it was time to put things into action. I began to break down old habits and change the routines that no longer worked for me. These things kept me very stagnant. They caused the same problems to arise and the same outcome.

I started writing. I always loved to write. I wrote little poetry in school (I learned how to in one of my elementary schools John Story Jenks). They taught me different forms of writing, especially poetry, and I fell in love with writing. I received a journal from a friend as a gift, and I wrote in it almost every day. It was a pink furry Minnie Mouse book. It had a big Minnie head on it, and when you pressed it, it had Minnie's giggle. This is when I learned how to release what I was feeling. I realized how it made me feel to write it down, and this helped me not stay stagnant. It helped me grow little by little. Growing feels uncomfortable; it doesn't feel good at all. Growing caused me to admit some things to myself and be accountable for things I didn't want to be. It's always easier to blame someone else or your circumstance. Growing means apologizing to those you hurt no matter how much time has passed. That frees you as well; trust me, try it!

I recently learned about fixed mindset vs. growth mindset. My husband asked me about it regarding myself, and once talking to him, I was intrigued to find out more. I found and listened to an audiobook by Carol S. Dweck PhD titled Mindset: The New Psychology of Success. I learned how much I had a fixed mindset but also how to change that mindset, if I wanted to. She gave different scenarios on both and how they would affect your life.

It taught me how a fixed mindset keeps you stagnant and how little you grow. It keeps you at cup half empty vs. looking at the cup half full.

I was always a half-empty cup person, and I refused for that to be. I wasn't enjoying life, I wasn't appreciating my growth, and where I was, I did not accept the little accomplishments. I was always waiting for the big one, the grand accomplishment. She explained a fixed mindset like this; it's when you're concerned with how you'll be judged, you're always trying to prove yourself, you're super sensitive about being wrong or even making mistakes, to name a few.

With a growth mindset, you focus on how you'll be improving, you believe important qualities can be cultivated, you don't mind obstacles, you actually prefer them, and you stretch yourself a bit. That's what I heard in my own words from her. The difference is you stay where you are and you're pretty much scared of change vs. you being open to change and the obstacles to overcome as you get there.

We grow in stages but make sure to process each stage as you grow through them. I acknowledged what it was that needed changing, I had to be honest with myself on if I was ready to change it or not. I sat in what I wanted to change and forgave those situations and people who kept me stagnant.

I actually wrote these things down and just read them, but I put them in a way where I already overcame them before I did, pretty much manifesting where I wanted to be. I forgave myself. I gave myself an okay to feel and to forgive. I moved on to how I wanted these things to change and what they would look like for me. Started off slow and took my time. I looked around me, and I placed people that's in my life in the circles they belonged in and made sure for me to hold myself accountable with them staying there. I appreciated my growth and made sure to sit in that.

Last, it was loving myself through every stage, which I learn how to do more of every single day, more today than I did even a year ago. I'm no longer being hard on myself, and I've forgiven myself. I respect what I have been through, and I am okay with where I am at. I am okay with who I used to be and embracing who I have grown to be.

These things didn't happen overnight some took days, months, but also years. It's still a process, honestly, and sometimes I slip, but the important part is to regroup, take accountability for where you are, how you slipped and get back to where you want to be.

Sometimes you may have to change course and try something different and that's okay as long as you're open for that new change leading to new growth. Practice these new traits, write yourself a letter, sticky notes on your mirror and/or even a vision board as reminders to who and what you want to be.

I've had a fixed mindset for so long that I had anxiety trying to reroute my mind into a growth mindset, but today I can say that my shoulders feel lighter. I feel free. I feel like I don't have to carry everyone, and I don't feel guilty about putting myself first. This growth mindset feels like I'm a whole new me, and I feel capable of taking on anything that is thrown my way. Looking forward to accomplishing all and anything I want in life.

If you've never heard of that book, please read or listen to it. it changed my life a lot.

Goal Setting

G oal setting help with life decisions and to brace yourself. When I set goals, I usually set them in time frames. I'll have goals for 24 hours, one week, one month, three months, six months, one year, three years (sometimes), five years and ten years. These change sometimes for me. If I didn't get things done by the time frame I planned, I move them down a little further or I add them back to another time frame that work for me.

I set goals so that I can keep myself accountable. They help me to not be all over the place and so that I don't get too frazzled day to day. I set the goals, I check them regularly and set my day up to achieve them.

My advice when it comes to goal setting is to give yourself some grace. I used to get so upset when I didn't achieve my goals in the time frame I put them in. It frustrated me so badly that I would not even focus on my other goals or recognize when I was making progress, not even the little accomplishments. It held me back, again, that fixed mindset. It was kind of like, oh this didn't work, so I know nothing else will, and once I learned that to not be the truth, it made me more successful in goal achieving.

One goal that I struggled a lot with was finances. I didn't grow up with anyone teaching me about finances. I had to learn them on my own. You know when I did? Three years ago.

I sat with my husband for a few years, going back on forth on plans that could work for me. I failed, and I failed. I went to my brother for help, and he gave me instructions on what to do, and I was lax. It took for me to literally be in a hole to buckle down and make something work.

My husband and I came up with a plan that worked, and I stuck with it and saw a big change. At that time, it worked for me, I had to eventually change it, but it did not get me down or keep me stuck like it once did. I broke that habit of being stuck and my goals being on hold because one thing didn't go as planned.

I set goals for my kids and marriage as well. Setting goals is no different than planning date night or planning to help your kids with their homework. Even planning dinner for the day or week is also a goal.

I make goals for myself individually, along with ones for us as a family. Success in my life all depended upon my goals. If I wake up and have nothing planned, I, personally, will be all over the place. Having these goals in place keeps me focused.

Get started; what are you waiting for? Start somewhere. What have you done to start goals and change your routine of not getting anything done? If not, start there. Figure out what timeline you want for your goals. Make them realistic. Be flexible. What you want them to be and how you want to achieve them. I'll go you one further, write your celebration goal. How will you celebrate the goal you have achieved? Even if it's as little as eating your favorite snack or having a solo dance party for ten minutes. Do it!

Dreams Deferred

Although you set goals in life, they can and will often change depending on your life circumstances. Just because you didn't get to live in it yet doesn't mean it isn't your dream. Sometimes our priorities change, and we have to put certain dreams on hold. As a young people sometimes, we don't know how to prioritize our dreams and what we want to do. Mine started when I chose to have my son instead of aborting him like my parents thought I should. They saw my future, so I get their reasoning, I just didn't feel like I wanted to do that.

I got an acceptance letter to Shippensburg University a few months prior to finding out I was pregnant. They offered me a scholarship as well. Since I can remember, I always earned great grades, and I was rewarded since grade school. I still had the mindset of going for nursing or forensic science. I just knew I wanted to be a Nurse on the Navy ship. I knew I wanted to do so many things, but I also knew I wanted to have my son and love up on him. I never had a doubt in my mind that I would be successful, even if things had to wait.

I finished High School after having my son. I went back to school even before my maternity leave was over. I was determined to finish high school. I made sure while I was out to get work and turn it in. I made sure that my dreams and my future stayed in the forefront of my mind; I was not only doing it for me but for my son too. He made all the difference for me to go harder; however, plans changed as to how I needed to go about things.

I enrolled in cosmetology school and went that route. That mobile hair salon was now my first dream. I wanted to get that up and rolling. My health got in the way of that, so again, dreams changed around. The Navy also came to a halt because of my documented health issues. At this point, I knew I had to go the entrepreneur way. That's just what I did.

I say all of this to say that a dream may be deferred, but that doesn't make you less successful. I would say pick up where you are, stay motivated, and never let those dreams die. Continue to reroute yourself if you need to, start over and even switch plans; just always keep going.

It's okay to take a break but get back to it. I believe in you. I have had so many plans since I was a kid. So many things I thought I would do. I refused to let any of my illnesses stop me from succeeding and caring properly for my children and myself. That's the mindset I love to keep always.

Every day I get up and push to be a better me. Every day I pray for better health. There are some days when I don't want to move. We will all have those days but push past them. What God has planned for us, we'll never know. Giving up is easy, take the not so easy road and fight, push through and stay positive.

Acceptance

I n life we often feel like our life is supposed to go a certain way, or we want it to go a certain way. We also feel like we have all the time in the world to forgive, love, and let go of the things that people have done to us, or we blame ourselves for. In the past few years, I have done so much for myself that I have been learning to love, forgive, let go of things and give it all to God all while growing. On September 26, 2017, at 9:45am I have to say that my life took a bit of a change, my maternal grandmother (the one who took raised me) passed away.

Although we didn't have a good bond growing up, the bond we grew was shocking yet good for us both, I would say. I saw this change start to unfold when I moved to Maryland. When I decided to move to Maryland, I only told about five people.

Everybody else found out when I was on the road leaving. My mother told me my mom-mom said she was going to miss me coming over or popping up. When I did come down to visit, she let me know she looked forward to me visiting again and that she loved me. Now mom-mom never said she loved me really, so I knew she meant it and missed us. Things were extremely clear for me when we had to be housed with each other again.

When I had surgery and had to move back with my mother. Later on, her health worsened and had to move in my mothers' home as well. Was I happy about this move? Absolutely not! But as time went on, I realized it wasn't bad and we weren't the same people we used to be years ago. Besides a few friends, she was really my biggest cheerleader. She made sure I didn't slack and encouraged me with kindness.

No, every day wasn't all good, but I mean, what adults don't clash? It was nothing like when I was younger. She gave me her support when I needed it, and I gave her the same. She began to trust me, and I did the same. She was there for me through my Left Total Hip Replacement Surgery. That surgery was different than any other one that I had in the past, and she was there to motivate me—made sure that I took my meds and drank plenty of water.

I knew she needed me as well because hospital visits and sickness became more frequent for her. I quickly pushed myself to heal so much, so I left therapy earlier than I should have. I helped my mother take care of my grandmother at night, and on days she had to work. The night shift was our shift together. From giving her meds when her finger or stomach hurt, putting her legs back on the bed when they slipped off, watching LMN, Greenleaf, Twilight or even Underworld. Down to her favorite commercial, the Gain detergent commercial, in which those memories will last a lifetime.

I say this to say no matter what relationship you may have had in the past with someone forgive yourself, forgive them and love them for who they are. You never know when they will need you and you will need them. I started to see so much of a change in mom-mom, or maybe I started understanding more and stop being so resentful. I witnessed her asking God for forgiveness and it was so genuine and detailed, she thought I was sleep and I was the only one in the room. That lightened my heart for her even more.

You never know when someone will be gone out of your life. I'm grateful I was given a chance to have a better relationship with my grand mom, even for that short period that we had. Nothing in the past mattered in those moments. Some days I do wish that I did it a while ago, but I believe God did it in the right allotted time because I had already been working on other relationships and giving others a chance to be more to me. I have expanded my mind and the way I think. I try not to get so agitated with people as fast as I used to. I'm gaining patience, forgiveness, love on a whole other level, and, most importantly gratitude!

Mom Mom, you are truly missed and loved. I pray you are resting peacefully.
Rest In Peace.

To Be Continued...

When I sit and look back at all the things that happened in my life, I can't help but think about how things could have been prevented, and truly God knows best! I know that the things I chose to do in my life have caused some of the outcomes of things I went through. Forcing relationships, beating myself up, abusing opioids, or even not loving myself, got me caught up in things I wasn't proud of and hindered me from my growth.

Sometimes when you're going through things in life, you don't understand why. You question, "Why me?" "Why did all of this have to happen?" "Why is this still happening?" "When will enough just be enough?"

What you don't realize is that what is meant to hit you won't pass you, and what's meant to pass you won't hit you. Everything in life has a purpose. Every struggle or test you've been through, will be your walking testimony. That's something my cousin Candice (Tee) used to tell me.

I can't say that I understood her when she said it but I'm beginning too now. Everything I have been through has made me the person I am today. You don't recognize your strength until you have no choice but to be strong. Until you're forced to get up and push. Until you are no longer just being strong for yourself and your children. Many have stated to me and assured me that it was my choice. That I could have easily chosen to quit and not push, not care about my children, to give up on everything. I continue to make that choice to keep pushing. I refuse to quit. It also made me have tough skin for the outside world.

Don't get me wrong; it still gets tough here and there. I still sometimes sit back and think about all that has happened to me. I try not to let it get me down as much anymore. I think about what positives I have gained from it and how I can somehow use it to help others.

I've repeatedly experienced people trying to dim my light. Look at me now, and it's just the beginning! If I can do it, so can you! Never give up on your dreams and goals. Push hard and never give up.

I've been 17, pregnant, and abused. I've undergone multiple surgeries, and I fight many other health issues daily. I am the epitome of a warrior. Fight and continue to push through each day. One thing I always say to myself is, "I can handle this, it could be worse." Each day I learn something new. Even with parenthood, every day you learn something brand new, young and older parents.

So, the present and future is moving forward for me with a positive mind and open heart. Giving my babies something that I lacked in being raised, which is unconditional love, care and time. As parents we learn new things all the time. Honestly, I feel like I'm recently just learning how to reciprocate love to them. How could I have done something that wasn't done around me? I learned and am learning so much through them. It's so amazing what they can teach you just by them being them.

For so long I never felt what love really was. Them loving me unconditionally, shows me how to love and how to accept it. Loving myself first and then others. When you don't love yourself, you give others room to take advantage of you and not really love you properly. Make sure that the love is equal or greater coming from the other person. Give everyone a fair chance but be aware that everyone won't love you the same, and that's okay. People are in your life for a reason, season, or lifetime. Everybody can't and won't be around forever.

Take responsibility for your actions. Don't just place the blame on others and not hold yourself accountable for what you have done. Think things through before making moves and acting on things. While I was young and even in my early adulthood, I can say I acted without thinking. I did this a lot. Don't play the blame game either. Some won't take accountability anyway so it's a waste of time. Plus, you're only responsible for YOU!

Moving forward I plan to take each day as it come. Love me every day through all my struggles and mishaps, even to celebrate and appreciate every single accomplishment and growth spurts big or small. I also want to know that nothing that has or will happen defines me and nothing is too big for me to handle. That breaking down, crying and taking a break is okay, for as long as I get back up and do what I'm supposed to do in life. To never permanently give up and not to sit in fear and failures. I've learned that those things hinder me from growing and that no matter how much I sit in negative thoughts and feelings the world still moves on.

I appreciate my life lessons. These things hit me for years straight. Sometimes with little breaks in between and sometimes it was back-to-back lessons and struggles. Through gaining and growing in my faith I found life to be grander. I now understand what it feels like to be one with myself, love God first, love and appreciate my life struggles and the blessings in all. I know that life won't be perfect and I'm sure that I will have many more trials and storms to get through.

Through these trials and storms to come I know that God promised me an end to death, sorrow and pain. I know that through strong faith I can conquer anything. I

My first example of a man's Love.
Rest In Peace, Grandpop Phil.

www.ingramcontent.com/pod-product-compliance
Lightning Source LLC
Chambersburg PA
CBHW071703210326
41597CB00017B/2312